wabi

QUIETNESS

kanso

seijaku

静

寂

SUBTLE

FRESH

寂

fukinsei

yugen

sabi

考

古

脱

shizen

自

然

NATURALNESS

ASYMMETRY

VENERABLE

俗

datsuzoku

datsuzoku

SURPRISE

SURPRISE

WITHDRAWN

GIBBS·SMITH
P
PUBLISHER

WABI SABI A New Look at Japanese Design

*with text and photographs
by Lennox Tierney*

For my wife, Catherine, and photographer son, Stephen.

With great appreciation to the publisher, Gibbs Smith; editor Gail Yngve;
and designer Kinde Nebeker, for the inspiration to proceed.
Thanks, however, are inadequate to my great teachers in Japan:
Kenji Yamanaka, Roshi Nakagawa, Dr. Soetsu Yanagi, Shoji Hamarla,
Sofu Teshigahara, and Kanjiro Kawai.

First Edition

02 01 00 99 4 3 2 1

Text and photographs © 1999 by Lennox Tierney

Published by
Gibbs Smith, Publisher
P.O. Box 667
Layton, UT 84041
Orders: (1-800) 748-5439
Visit our Web site at www.gibbs-smith.com

Designer: Kinde Nebeker
Editor: Gail Yngve

Printed in Asia
Library of Congress Catologing-in-Publication Data

Tierney, Lennox.
　　　　　Wabi sabi / Lennox Tierney.
　　　　　　　　　　p.　cm.
　　　　　ISBN 0-87905-849-8
　　　　　1. Design—Japan—Themes, motives.　2. Zen Buddhism—Influence.
　　I. Title.
　　NK1484.A1T54　1999
　　745.4'4952—dc21
　　　　　　　　　　　　　　　　　　　　　　　　　99–25659
　　　　　　　　　　　　　　　　　　　　　　　　　　　　　CIP

THE QUEST

Arriving in Japan as a neophyte
Westerner with my newly acquired
knowledge of textbook Japanese,
I was all questions.

As part of the military government of Japan after World War II—entitled to an automobile and gasoline in a war–ravaged nation bereft of such luxuries—I was able to travel around the country. Immediately surrounded by unfamiliar situations, places, and customs, the questioning side of life loomed large on the horizon. My first impulse was typically American: get into the car and drive somewhere.

This inn's welcoming path, or roji, leads to the entry in a wall of black plaster that lends distance to the small space.

In Kyoto, the old capital city of
Japan that was well preserved and
free from bombing during World
War II, my goal was to visit the
famous stone garden of the
Ryoanji in the northern sector of
the city. I had read about this
garden and was intrigued by the
notion of a garden without
visible plants—the first of many
Japanese puzzles I would discover.
Pointing the nose of the 1939
Mercury (the only such vehicle in
Japan) north, I arrived in the
general vicinity of my objective.

The placement of stones
in this kyusho garden
is at once spontaneous
and studied. Raked white
sand echoes the shapes of
the rocks, anchoring them
visually in place, as well
as creating a sense of
fluid motion — like water
around islands in the sea.

He stopped and gazed intently at this amazing sight—a foreigner in an automobile. Then, looking at me quizzically, he politely responded to my question. He said the temple was far, far away. When I showed him my map indicating that the temple was nearby, he said, "It is just around the corner; it is far away only for people with blue eyes." Saying this, he then resumed his travel.

Lesson one had just occurred. I was a *gaijin* (foreign barbarian); therefore, I was ignorant as to why the garden was created.

After driving aimlessly through a series of maze-like streets, my first lesson in an important Asian concept occurred. Lost and frustrated, upon seeing an elderly man quietly pedal by on an ancient bicycle, I stopped the car. In my best textbook Japanese, I asked him for directions.

Upon reaching my destination, I met a kindly monk within the monastery who enlightened me on the basic Zen principles of *fukinsei* and *kanso* (asymmetry and simplicity).

The ancient tradition of Buddhist monks in Japanese society dates back hundreds of years. A greater percentage of young men have at least some experience of the spiritual life of a monastery than in the West, and many will dedicate their whole lives to spiritual practice.

fukinsei ASYMMETRY

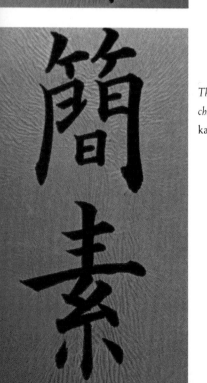

kanso SIMPLICITY

This knowledge was shared over cups of green tea, and I was given time to meditate on the famous garden: fifteen stones asymmetrically set in flat, carefully raked white sand with no evidence of larger plants. In reality, the rocks were home to nearly invisible colonies of lichens, yet the irregularly placed stones seemed so extreme without visible plants. No wonder foreigners often did not appreciate their understated simplicity.

The Ryoanji Temple dry garden.

The twisting gnarled roots of this great tree inspire wonder and provoke admiration for its great and venerable age.

Lesson number two took place one fine day in autumn as I walked along the shore of Lake Kasumi ga ike, located in the Kenroku-en Garden in Kanazawa. An ancient pine tree loomed large, with its huge exposed roots splayed across the surrounding earth. As I took a photograph of this sight, Japanese journalists, all carrying cameras, approached and demanded to know the reason for my interest in photographing the roots of the pine. In contrast, I was amazed that they were photographing me at a seeming inopportune time.

9

The Japanese characters for koko

koko AUSTERE

Again, a Buddhist monk brought enlightenment to the scene. Overhearing the conversation, he volunteered the answer, stating simply that I must be intrigued by the *koko* (austere) principle aspect of the old pine's roots that indicated its great and venerable age. All the journalists and other visitors then entered into a discussion of yet another defining and related concept—*sabi* (objects that are

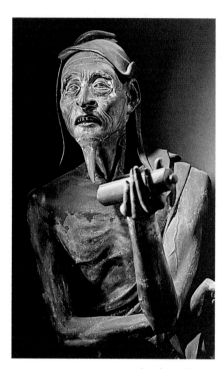

Age portrayed in this sculpture's form (sagging skin, protruding bones) combines with the age of its material, a peeling dark-lacquer surface, to create a particular kind of beauty that only comes with great age.

venerable and beautiful because of their patina of age). Sabi often is found with its opposite, *wabi* (the beauty inherent in fresh newness). The monk suggested that I must be fascinated by the koko and the sabi, which were characteristic of the roots. Having never before encountered these aspects, I innocently agreed and immediately acquired the concepts that would be useful for future observations of the works of nature and humankind.

An artistic sign on a Japanese shop beautifully displays an ancient Japanese coin, characteristic of sabi.

The fresh temporal beauty of a purple iris, characteristic of wabi.

The simplicity of the Korakuen Garden in Okayama is both arresting and austere.

My encounter led me on a quest for the other part of the term— *wabi*. This time my path led to the second of the three greatest gardens of Japan—the Korakuen in Okayama. There in that garden was a pond, and in that pond was an island of pure white sand. Growing in the sand was a solitary bonsai pine. The simplicity of the scene was arresting, and it embodied the spirit of what the Buddhist monk called kanso. It also represented the clean-cut beauty of the wabi concept.

The modern architectural lines of this Tokyo cathedral embody aspects of wabi.

Different facets of the amazing puzzle were now falling into place. I was developing a new language for art analysis, which was an exciting and humbling experience, arriving as it did, after a proper Western university training in the arts.

Cherry blossom—laden boughs frame the graceful roofs of a Japanese pagoda.

Deeper in that beautiful garden was a grove of blossoming cherry trees. There, I experienced yet another aspect of my new enlightenment. Several rural families were sitting in a circle under the tree branches and drinking warm *sake* (rice wine) poured into tiny cups from porcelain "singing" sake bottles that chirped like birds during the frequent pourings. A gusty breeze was causing a veritable snowstorm of cherry petals to swirl around the group. Seeing me, a kindly, elderly woman rose and approached.

Sensing that I was a gaijin standing alone outside the circle, she insisted, in a wonderful country accent, that I join the group for warm rice wine and relax in the "spring snow" of cherry petals. Then, I realized that sabi pertains to people and occasions, as well as to things and events relating to fleeting moments of beauty, hence, the inherent sadness of sabi and the "here today, gone tomorrow" aspect of it. The falling petals dramatized the fleeting moment of beauty and the temporary aspect of nature itself. Here was another enlightenment, one that related to the beauty of nature achieved through a spontaneous and perfectly natural process.

A stone lantern, found often in Japanese gardens, wears a living hat of moss and lichens.

Open-armed doors
of a Japanese inn.

A further intriguing aspect was evident in the ever-present subtlety of most things traditionally Japanese. Seeking an answer to this phenomenon brought me to a *ryokan* (inn) on the island of Shikoku, located in the inland Sea of Japan. Upon our arrival by boat in a torrential rain, the scene was

gray and muted in color. My wife
and I were taken to the old section
of Takamatsu, where we expected to
stay overnight at an inn before
moving farther inland. The Ka Sen
Villa Inn was small, quiet, and
unpretentious. Our room's sliding
shoji screens opened onto an
exquisite small garden, drenched in
the continuous downpour. At dusk,
a maid wearing a straw rain cape lit
a stone lantern—the only warm
color noted in this gray palette.

*It was raining and dusk when
the stone lantern was lit—
the only warm color in a
palette of gray-greens.*

Relaxing on *zabuton* (pillows) by the soft glow of the coals from the hibachi charcoal burner, we marveled at how exciting the unexpected could be. Searching for the subtlety of this serene atmosphere, I turned to the *daijiten* (Japanese dictionary), where I found the term *yugen* (mystery, profundity, occult, subtle, abstruse). So, there it was, an additional principle of Zen—yugen subtly controlled the scene and the occasion.

Misty ocean weather of the islands of Japan and along the river Li in south China creates a feeling of delicate mystery that is common to the arts of both Japan and China.

Quiet color and geometric simplicity are seen in this floor of tatami *mats.*

The quietly reserved guest room of the Ka Sen Villa Inn is inviting to weary travelers.

The objects in the room exhibited restrained color—the straw *tatami* (floor mats), the dark blue of the hibachi, and the strangely muted color (produced by mixing powdered seaweed into plaster) of the *tokonoma* (an alcove that held a scroll painting and a flower arrangement). Colors of this nature, as in all things of great restraint, may be referred to as *shibui* (greatly reserved, astringent, sober, quiet).

The beauty, serenity, and mystery
of a Japanese landscape captivates
the sensitive eye and heart.

20

Our overnight visit turned into a weeklong stay because my wife and I could not bring ourselves to leave this magic place of ultimate, quiet serenity. Rain was never more beautiful or even musical as the waterfall chains on the roof's drains turned into a melodic accompaniment to daily living. Our plans for a few days of inland travel vanished in order for us to savor the magic room and garden at Ka Sen Villa with its ultimately profound subtleties.

Twilight and rain enhance the beauty of the Ka Sen Villa garden.

One fine late summer evening, another lesson in the meaning of yugen occurred, which further enforced my understanding of another facet in the jewel of enlightenment needed to fathom this amazing culture. After stopping at a ryokan and taking a hot springs bath, it was time to retire. However, I first opened the shoji panels to a small garden that contained an enormous lichen-covered stone above a small pool where koi fish swam silently in the dark water. Water musically fell drop by drop through a bamboo pipe into a water cricket, a bamboo tube that is alternately filled and emptied by gravity, spilling the water into the pond and striking a sounding stone with a resounding tone. This device was originally used to frighten away badgers that would come to fish by the light of the full moon.

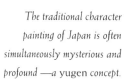

The traditional character painting of Japan is often simultaneously mysterious and profound —a yugen concept.

The scene depicted here is an excellent example of a green gauze room often found in Japan's country inns.

The maid soon came and quietly closed the shoji, blocking off the view of the garden and enclosing the room in an atmosphere that the Japanese refer to as *kojin mari* (coziness). Next, she brought a large square fold of green gauze netting and attached it by rope to a brass ring in the center of the low ceiling. The corners were attached to additional rings, and then by pulling on the center cord, as if by magic, a room within a room appeared, made of green mosquito netting bound at the top and

24

corners by vermilion felt, the color used by country inns. (City inns use blue felt and shaded blue netting.) The futon was prepared inside with a small *andon* (lamp) placed beside it. One entered this inner sanctum to sleep in peace and serenity after first receiving a massage from a blind masseuse. (In Japan, the blind are cared for their entire lives by inn owners in exchange for this service.) Once the masseuse departed, the maid brought a small cage filled with fireflies and released them inside the netted room. Then she extinguished the andon and the room was dark for a

few moments until the starlight illuminating the round moon window made its exquisite form subtly visible.

The moon window provides the symmetrical contrast to the asymmetrical aspects of most Japanese art forms.

At the inn, I once again experienced yugen, the principle relating to things that are suggested rather than totally revealed.

This inn literally had provided a symphony of subtleties, which made yugen a part of one's total enlightenment.

The cedar ceiling of the Samurai Inn was pure architectural deception—functional in its purpose of tricking the enemies of the guests.

Sadly, as Japan enters a new millennium, it has, for the most part, exchanged these centuries-old customs for the convenience of air conditioning and noisy forced-air ventilation, together with their debilitating noise and pollution.

This solemn priest is of the Grand Shinto shrine at Ise.

On another of my journeys (this time to a little-known temple shrine high in the Japanese mountains that included a stay at an inn in the village of Myogi), I was to find another Zen principle. Earlier in the day, we had visited the vicinity and discovered a group of venerable and nearly deserted shrines and temples in the foothills of Mount Myogi. Since it was November, the maple trees were ablaze with crimson, known in Japan at that time of year as Momiji. After thoroughly exploring the area, we arrived at the inn by late afternoon, thoroughly chilled.

My wife and I warmed ourselves, first with tea and then with the steaming baths from the inn's *onsen* (hot springs).

The natural settings of many of Japan's structures impart drama and a strong sense of place, as in this alternate site for the rebuilding every twenty years of the Grand Shinto Shrine at Ise.

After supper, I dressed warmly and returned alone to the shrines in order to observe them by full moon. The contrast of the deep black shadows and the light of the brilliant moon was breathtaking. This lonely experience was silent and eerie, made all the more so by a peculiar sense that overwhelms an individual when feeling the presence of another unseen human being. Standing in that ancient temple court, I recognized the Zen principle I was seeking—*seijaku* (solitude). The stillness and tranquillity of that place created a transcendent moment.

Tall chryptomeria trees are protectively wrapped as a sign of respect.

The Japanese characters for seijaku

A Japanese garden is filled with symbols of all the Zen principles as well as ones relative to nature in the suggestions of cliffs, streams, and forest glades.

Early the next morning as I descended through the mist into the village, I encountered a woodcutter chopping pine branches for a fire. The night before, he had seen me enter the temple court.

Since I was alone and a Westerner, he mentioned that he was concerned I might fall or become cold, so he had sent his young son

The symbolism of rippling water can be seen in the roof tiles of a temple.

to watch over me, advising him to stay out of sight so as not to disturb my tranquillity within that ancient place. Another seijaku moment had occurred.

It is fair to say "things Japanese" are often an analysis—a combination of complexities involving more than one principle or concept that is foreign to Westerners. Understanding these matters requires an enlightenment at a higher realm—one that is truly cultural in its breadth. No wonder the gaijin is often perplexed at first contact with these complexities.

Increasingly evident in my travels and contacts in Japan was a naturalness in most everything I saw and sensed. Nature was seemingly everywhere, even in this densely populated country of compact housing and congested pathways.

Again, my Buddhist monk friends were able to identify an underlying principle at work— *shizen* (naturalness in all things). Manmade and artificial materials are the opposite of this concept.

shizen NATURALNESS

The Japanese characters for shizen

A natural bend in the sacred Isuzu River that flows through Ise Shrine is a classic example of shizen.

I was aware of shizen in the *ikebana* (flower arrangement) found in every room's tokonoma where nature is brought into close view for all individuals.

An example of ikebana, or flower arrangement, brightens this tokonoma.

33

Finding that everyone in Japan was as literate about ikebana as Westerners are about spoken language impressed me. Everyone seemed to know about the flowers and plants of the four seasons. Even bus drivers and train engineers could not work without an ikebana nearby. One more piece of the puzzle was falling into place to help me read this amazing culture, different from Western culture in so many ways. Shizen was a necessary link and an important piece in the jigsaw that was forming in my mind.

A chabana, or tea master's flower arrangement, is never ostentatious, displaying only a few garden flowers from the season.

At last I was able to appreciate the ikebana seen throughout the country. Indeed, it was a universally practiced folk art that mirrored human life and seasonal events. The *moribana* style uses a low container that shows much water (the yin or feminine element in the eternal opposites of yin and yang) with seasonal flowers in a triangle representing heaven, humankind, and earth. *Nageire* arrangements glorify and "legalize" the art of the casual, instantly creative, thrown-in style. The *rikka* style is a large complex statement that represents plants of all the seasons in a formal and classic way, suggestive of a temple and its sacred confines, where such arrangements were originally used. A similar adaptation of this classic form is found in the *seika* style, which is used for everyday arrangements. A tea master (master of the aesthetic environment typical of tea ceremonies) will arrange a single flower and bud from a home garden in a style referred to as *chabana*. This style is the ultimate statement in naturalness and simplicity.

A chabana of three plants is in a reserved-looking container for a tea ceremony.

The serenity of seijaku is apparent
in the great and small gardens of Japan,
which are always important parts of
private homes, inns, and geisha houses.

One of my most intense seijaku experiences occurred at the end of World War II. There is no silence like the silence of the doomed, and therein hangs a tale. During the post–World War II occupation of Japan, the geisha institution was misinterpreted by the occupiers who confused it with prostitution. In reality, geishas are Japanese women trained from childhood to be entertainers. The houses of geishas were beautiful and often of great historic and aesthetic value. One of my jobs during the occupation was to help draft a regulation that forbade entry into geisha houses by occupation personnel. The purpose of this proclamation was not only to protect the houses from the desecration of muddy boots on the fine straw tatami mats, but, more specifically, to protect the geishas from the unwanted attention of uninvited guests.

One day, however, I found myself in a difficult situation.

Nothing beautiful is ever lost in Japan. Here, ancient roof tiles are imbedded in a wall to create a rhythmic pattern.

A dinner setting of unmatched dishes is a fukinsei concept.

The great day arrived. I was seated at the right hand of the head geisha as a great feast was served in a room resplendent with magnificent works of art.

At the height of the banquet, a dreadful sound was heard — that of military Jeeps roaring into the courtyard. I froze in fear as I heard the heavy footfalls enter the building, rise on the stairs, and march through the hallways. Scarcely comforting were the whispered words of the head geisha, "Have no fear," for historically they were trained to reassure their samurai guests with such words just before their heads would roll.

I had received an invitation from my friend Kenji Yamanaka to a splendid occasion that was to take place at a famous geisha house at Omiya, a town north of Tokyo. Demurring, I reminded Kenji of the regulation. Finally, he prevailed upon me to dress in a kimono and travel in a native taxi, using the theory that only Japanese visited this house.

The palms of my hands were clammy as I contemplated the headlines in the next day's edition of the *Stars and Stripes*. My most vivid memory was the terrifying silence in the room. Seijaku never was more evident.

Then, it all died away as the Jeeps roared out of earshot and the head geisha turned to me to say, "You see, there was nothing to worry about."

Turning to my host, I asked, "To what do I owe this amazing deliverance?" Kenji told me that geisha houses were designed for just such circumstances.

This beautiful room was a "puzzle room" built in such a way as to deceive intruders, who would wrongly assume they had examined every room, when in reality, they had not.

The flexibility of traditional Japanese architecture is apparent in these room areas that employ sliding panels to divide the space in different ways.

ARTISTIC CREATIVITY

Intrigued by the artistic creativity so prominent in Japan and curious as to the ultimate controlling principle, I was led on a search for this illusive yet fundamental principium.

Zen monks identified it for me as *datzuzoku* (an astonishing surprise). This artistry was an unexpected and transcendent experience, resulting from contact with something creative in its nature.

Incompleteness of subject placement often leads to abstraction in the two-dimensional arts; this has influenced the West where abstraction has flourished in the last century.

41

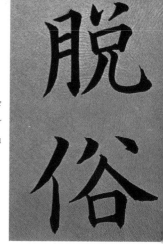

A hot summer day provided an event that illustrated this principle. Roshi Nakagawa, the head monk of the Ryutakuji (Zen monastery) at Mishima was entertaining several of my American friends and me.

Japanese prints usually surprise Westerners with their nonoptical perspective, creative uses of color and pattern, and unconventional placement of subject matter.

This simmering day took place in *Doyo* (one of the eleven hottest days of summer). We climbed several flights of steps to a large matted room high in the leafy treetops. Though open on four sides, the heat and humidity were oppressive. We sat with the *roshi* on *zabuton* (straw floor cushions), and in the center of our circle was a large white porcelain bowl that held a veritable mountain of ice. A cave-like depression in this ice mountain held the globular head of a giant blue hydrangea blossom— its color reflected through the fractures in the ice.

The famous painter Mu Chi paints five persimmons in an economy of black ink strokes. The color is felt without being seen.

43

While we contemplated the stillness and the heat, Roshi Nakagawa took a large leaf fan and slowly fanned us. Suddenly, a calm stillness descended upon the stifling room, and it seemed strangely cool. A question arose in the conversation relative to my imminent return to the United States. Was there a message the roshi would like to send with me? Silently, Roshi Nakagawa took an artist's brush and in exquisite calligraphy brushed a message on the leaf fan that said "fan others." Then he gave me the fan to carry on my journey. The ultimate creativity of the flower inside the mountain of ice and the soothing coolness of the fanning illustrated the concept of datzuzoku.

A miroku, or Buddha of the future.

By now, I had accumulated a set of principles and a vocabulary useful in coming to terms with the East-versus-West cultural riddle. I had experienced fukinsei (asymmetry), kanso (simplicity), koko (austerity), shizen (naturalness), yugen (subtlety), seijaku (solitude), and now the illusive datzuzoku.

For Western civilization, the accompanying concepts of wabi, sabi, and shibui rounded out a new evaluation of the arts and the cultures that produced them.

This ornate rusted-iron hinge is found on an ancient castle gate.

THE TEA CEREMONY

The one ritual that best summarizes all the experiences of Japanese culture is the tea ceremony, which involves every aspect of the concepts discussed herein. This is a lay, yet seemingly religious, ceremonial serving of tea under carefully controlled conditions—a kind of communion of aesthetics resulting in a *satori* (instant enlightenment) for the attending guests.

The open form of this haresfur *tea bowl indicates that it is for summer tea ceremony—open to release the heat of the tea. Tea bowls are seasonal in character, from closed for winter to straight-sided for spring and fall.*

In *The Art of Taking Tea*, Sen Soshitsu quoted the Buddhist monk Murata Shuko, who was probably the originator of *cha-no-yu* (hot water for tea), as saying: "It is not an amusement, nor a technique either, but an enjoyment of enlightened satisfaction."

Sen no Rikyu, founder of the tea ceremony as it is currently known in Japan, noted that the four governing principles of cha-no-yu are harmony, respect, purity, and tranquillity. He stated: "Make the water boil. Then prepare the tea . . . and drink. That is all to cha-no-yu." In the early twentieth century, Okakura Kakuzo said: "Cha-no-yu is a whole point of view about man and nature." It is a case of harmony with nature rather than against it.

A bamboo window grill of a teahouse, and a sliding paper-covered shoji give a soft and beautiful light by day and eliminate the blackness of night when closed in the evening.

A pinnacle of enlightenment is perhaps reached in the tea ceremony of Japan, where art and religion are practically synonymous. The ceremony may be experienced either in actuality or through literary association. The actual experience best takes place with a practiced and knowledgeable tea master in Japan or abroad in an environment conducive to satori. Sen Soshitsu said that the ceremony is a mental discipline meant to "satisfy a spiritual thirst . . . moistening a dry life."

Only recently have Western artists experimented with works of art in which the entire environment is involved in the expression. In it, the floor, walls, ceiling, room contents, lighting, and sound effects are all included. Observers are expected to achieve an immediate and ultimate understanding of the artist's intent and purpose—satori.

In cha-no-yu, this environment concept is of long-standing existence and tradition. It always physically embodied the floor, walls, ceiling, lighting, sound, taste, fragrance, and furnishings of a special room in a unique structure built for the purpose.
It is situated in a *cha niwa* (special garden) created by the tea master or mistress as a retreat from the work-a-day world and related to the function of the teahouse and its ceremony. As early as the seventeenth century, the tea masters or mistresses found their interests in spheres that were apart from the ordinary spheres of life and remote from the dust of this world.

The nijiri guchi, *or "wriggle-in"*
entrance, of a teahouse humbles all
before the ceremony begins.

Pictured are the accessories for a summer tea ceremony.

The ceremony embodies and exemplifies the concepts previously introduced and brings them into sensory recognition without literary explanation. This latter point is of great importance since the West stresses the written word and the literary association. Thus, in Japan, the tea ceremony becomes the final arbiter of good taste, elegance, form and function, and the essence of an intuitive understanding of things not easily defined in Western terms. This environment includes examples of all the arts, crafts, and architectural elements found in everyday life within a carefully composed atmosphere. No judgment is made as to whether something is good or bad. It is simply a near-perfect orchestration of sights, sounds, textures, colors, tastes, and fragrances that naturally delight the human senses and need no formal or literary explanations.

All of this is achieved through utmost simplicity with no attempt at ostentation or show. Yoshido Kenko notes from a twelfth- or thirteenth-century document: "Strange and rare things are mostly what amuse people of bad breeding.

A desire for curious things, a fondness for uncommon opinions is a sure characteristic of people of shallow understanding."

A tea master once told his young son to rake the path, which he did to perfection. Not a leaf was left in sight. Seeing this, his father shook the trees to produce this effect and said, "Now it's ready for the guests."

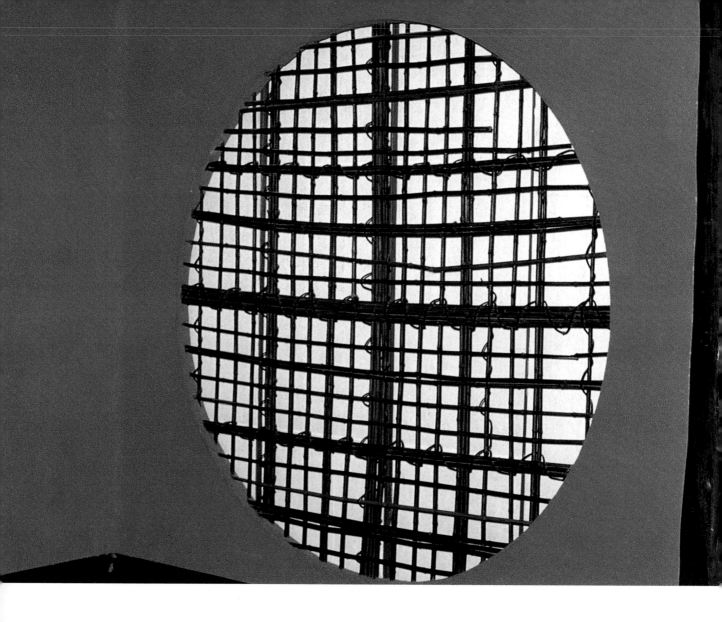

This single plant garden is the ultimate in reservation.

The teahouse is called the tea hut to insure its humility and is made of simple common materials. The hut actually is a mat-covered room in a rustic yet elegant structure within the confines of its own small garden. It must have no palatial aspects, so its garden is small and composed of seasonal plants indigenous to the area and restricted in number. The numbers should always be uneven—for example, three, five, seven, nine, eleven—with lower numbers preferable to higher ones. One-plant gardens often are found in cha niwa. In all cases, a plant "zoo" must be avoided. The secluded and understated Tai-an in Kyoto, designed by the great tea master Rikyu (1520–1591) is probably the best example of the classic architecture connected with the tea ceremony.

The *nijiri-guchi* (entryway) to the teahouse must be low so that all guests, regardless of status, must fall to their knees, bow, and, in doing so, experience actual and physical humility. Near the entrance, a *hishaku* (dipper) that is part of a beautiful and functional *tsukubai* (water basin), is used to wash the hands as a cleansing ritual before entering. Any extra drops of water are shared with a fern planted near the basin, symbolizing compassion and compatibility with nature. Parallel with this thought, Pablo Picasso, in an interview with Christian Zerves, provided a Western interpretation of nature: "One cannot oppose nature. It is stronger than the strongest of men! We all have an interest in being on good terms with her. We can permit ourselves some liberties, but only in detail."

A tsukubai is used for washing the face and hands before a tea ceremony.

A sheltered waiting place allows guests to contemplate peacefully before taking part in a tea ceremony.

A sheltered waiting place is provided for quiet meditation and for shedding the dust of the world. From this place, the guest is called by a melodious bell rung by the tea master after a proper period of peaceful contemplation and solitude. The guests, usually five in number, dress in a conservative fashion.

Invitations often are in brushed calligraphy on small folding fans made especially for this purpose and sent not less than three days in advance of the occasion. The Japanese post office delivers the stamped fans as regular mail.

The hours for a tea ceremony vary. Usually, dawn is the most formal time of the day, while evening is next. However, the most formal hour of the year is dusk on the evening of the full harvest moon.

This tea whisk is made from one finely split piece of bamboo.

Finally, when all is carefully inspected and an atmosphere of perfect coordination of all aspects is attained, the leader and others are called to the tearoom and the *Shokyaku* (lead guest) must perform the rituals in concert with the beauty and perfection intended. If for any reason an error is made, it must be carefully duplicated in turn by each of the following guests to avoid embarrassing the leader.

Here the Roshi, or abbot, of Ryutakuji Zen monastery invites us to a tea ceremony.

But, it is interesting to note that a considerable body of knowledge of the arts and of aesthetics is usually brought by the lead guest to the occasion. The other guests, if not equally enlightened, are then in position for a direct learning experience with regard to the understandings of architecture (the building), landscape and plants (the garden), social amenities (the group), painting (the scroll in the tokonoma), craftsmanship (the teacups and objects used in the ceremony), ikebana (the flower arrangement), music (the bell and insect sounds), fragrance (the incense), taste (the tea and cakes), poetry (room dedication board or poetry papers tied to wind bells in the garden), and calligraphy (the invitations, room dedication, or a scroll in the tokonoma). The learning experience is direct rather than vicarious, becoming part of an individual's native intuition rather than part of his or her intellectual baggage. All artificiality and unnaturalness is to be avoided and each article is an object of art in itself and should be appreciated (*haiken*) as part of an integrated whole.

Colorful and intricately designed tea cakes
are to be eaten as part of the tea ceremony.
They reflect either the occasion or the
seasons in their colors and forms.

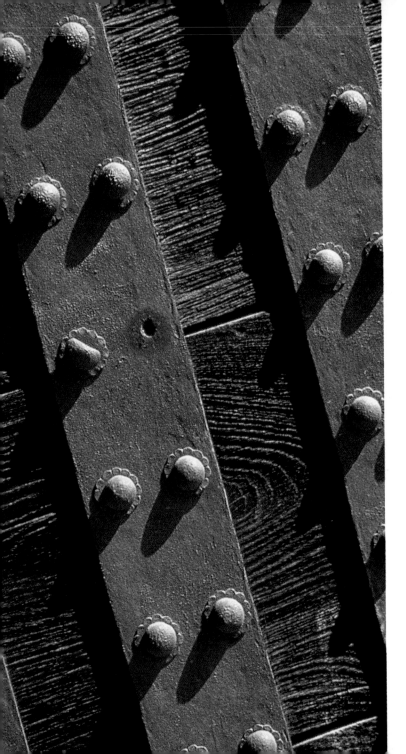

To paraphrase Sen no Rikyu, the way of tea utilizes the marvelous workings of the universal mind. In other words, an illustrious guest must shed his magnificence to become "a guest above the clouds." There are only host, guest, and tea.

One particular tea ceremony I attended serves to illustrate all or most of the foregoing concepts.

Red maple leaves delight guests of a tea ceremony.

The time was dusk of the harvest moon; the place was the garden and teahouse of a famous tea master, Mr. Mioshi. I was the Shokyaku, and the four other guests were all well-known tea masters in their own right.

A quiet seijaku *moment is discovered by a pond with stone lantern and* suitsuki, *or moon water grass.*

I arrived at the precise invitational time, parking my automobile a mile away in order to avoid any disturbance in the immediate neighborhood. The outer gate was standing slightly ajar, an indication that guests were expected. The garden path was mossy and moist, and its stones wet, a sign of immediate hospitality and careful concern for the guests on the part of the host. The *roji* (path) means the "dewed ground." The idea comes from a Buddhist Sutra (scripture), which states, "One stands on the white-dewed ground after leaving this world of flaming passions."

A feeling of freshness, as after a light rain shower, set the mood as guests proceeded to the *machiai*, (gathering place) where they assembled. The path is best appreciated when light rain moistens the stones.

The main stop along the roji was the tsukubai where guests used the beautifully crafted hishaku, which was found lying across the tsukubai, but, according to custom, should never divide the space in half.

A bronze basin such as this one was likely the original mirror. This basin, filled with rainwater, quietly reflects the scene above it.

A large stone lantern
exemplifies the Zen principle
of fukinsei, *or asymmetry.*

The cleansing ritual is a symbol of purification derived from Shinto tradition, and, as it took place, the guests were in a position to admire the surroundings of the basin as well as the composition of rocks, plants, and stone lantern in its vicinity.

This composition is from the art of the *niwa* (Japanese garden) and is one of the delights of personal attendance at a tea ceremony. The word *niwa* also translates to "pure place," with a garden being symbolic of a pure and undefiled space where one attains composure of the mind. The garden elements, consisting of air, earth, water, and fire, are symbolized in the invisible but life-sustaining air, the earth in the stones, the water in the tsukubai, the fire in the stone lantern, and the candles that were carried by all the guests in fine bronze candleholders.

To quote a Western proverb: "It is the exception that proves the rule." Here the straight-line path contrasts and emphasizes the rough irregularity of the other stones.

This scroll painting of sprouting bamboo is a seasonal reference to spring and the month of May.

The guests then proceeded through the *shiori-do* (inner gate) to the *koshikake* (arbor), where they were seated on round straw zabuton to await the host and the signal to enter the *chashitsu* (tearoom). At the sound of a gong, the guests entered through the nijiri-guchi, which required them to pass through the entrance by bowing their heads and crawling on their knees. Once inside, I *haikened* (appreciated) the tokonoma and its art objects—namely, the scroll and the ikebana.

The simple minimalism characteristic of Japanese design is evident in this tokomona with its scroll and ikebana.

The next stage of this particular tea ceremony was crucial. I bowed in the *shin* (formal) style before the white scroll, which was blank—completely devoid of calligraphy or other art. Etiquette demanded an appreciative statement relative to the content, artist, and/or history of the scroll. As Shokyaku, I was deeply puzzled by this unusual circumstance and at a loss as to how to properly react. I could not believe that a joke was being played on me as this would be entirely improper and out of character.

Silently, I was praying for a satori, which fortunately dawned on me. Since nothing was there, I said nothing. I made a small insignificant remark about the one white camellia and bud in an overturned roof tile within the tokonoma and then went on to haiken the bronze *furo* (brazier) and *kama* (iron kettle), which I recognized as to style and maker. I gradually began to realize why I was the Shokyaku in this rare company of famous tea masters. The ceremony, literally, was the Eastern equivalent of a doctoral dissertation, similar to that conducted in an American university.

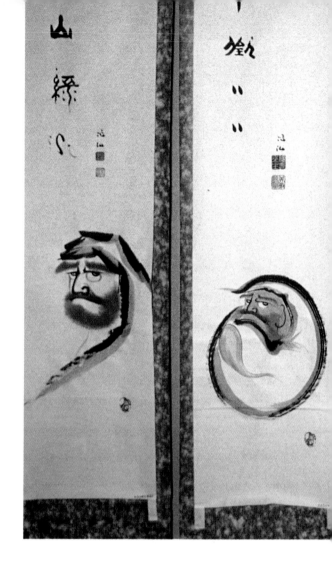

My answers, actions, and reactions were duly noted by a peer group with rare qualifications.

Daruma, one of the great saints of Buddhism, is depicted in several poses—all expressing the Zen principle of datsuzoku, *or creative surprise.*

One of the great masters of datsuzoku
(surprise) is the famous block printmaker
Sharaku. Depicted here is the character
of a great actor.

The *Chajin* (tea master) then called to one of his beautiful daughters who entered, dressed in a Heian-period kimono in deference to my principal research period of Japanese history at that time. The tea master picked up the tile with the one white camellia and bud from the tokonoma and poured out the water into the wastewater jar. Next, his daughter spread a handsome mat containing the seven beautiful grasses of autumn. Another daughter brought a Korean Koryo–dynasty gray celadon bottle with a high neck and placed it in the tokonoma.

An ikebana arrangement of great scale was created by Sofu Teshigahara in the nageire style.

With apparent abandon, the tea master then picked up the stalks of *suitsuki* (moon, water, grass) and other grasses, and with the slightest of glances, placed them into the bottle. This was to honor my interests in the nageire, thrown in the style of ikebana, which stresses the casual, unstudied, and instantly creative datsuzoku school of flower arrangement. A third daughter removed the simple arrangement and the mats, and all was serene with an exquisite new arrangement.

This basket of tea cakes is an example of pastries made for an autumn tea ceremony.

The ceremony proceeded with distribution of cakes, first to me, and then, during the *otemae* (the preparation of the tea), to the other guests, ending with the *tsume* (last guest). Just before serving the *koicha* (thick tea for formal ceremonies) in a *raku* (tea bowl) from the hand and mind of the great ceramic artist Koetsu, the Chajin asked us to extinguish candles, creating a darkness that was intensely black. One of the delights of the dark period was the gradually increasing awareness and vision of the glowing charcoal in the furo. A subtle musical note emanated from the container made by steel disks of various sizes with thin edges that vibrate in the boiling water, producing a symphonic sound in the solitude of the darkness, which is likened to the sighing of wind in the pine trees.

A light snow during the night transformed the famous Zen stone garden of Ryoanji into a fine black-and-white ink painting.

By the faint light from the charcoal, the Chajin moved across the room to a point out of sight of the guests. (It should be noted that chashitsu used for formal tea ceremonies have a thick, thatched roof through which a movable trapdoor is cut.) The Chajin then raised the door to an open position. It now was the hour of the full harvest moon that shone through the roof into the tokonoma, casting the grass shadows in an indescribably beautiful ink painting onto the snowy white *kakemono* (scroll). This was the purest essence of *sumi-e* (ink painting).

Exquisite beyond usual human
accomplishment, it was sublime
in its revelation of the beauty
of grasses in the moonlight.
My mentors, knowing that I
was a student of sumi-e,
demonstrated its most truthful
characteristics to me in an
arresting moment of satori.

*An ink painting catches
the essence of nature in
the wild.*

The Chajin then asked us to relight our candles and the ceremony proceeded to its conclusion after a haiken of the tea caddy and tea scoop. He expressed his thanks to the guests, and the guests expressed their gratitude to him. They departed via the nijiri-guchi. The tsume, being last, closed and latched the entryway. The guests, walking on the roji, paused and turned toward the nijiri-guchi, which the host opened as he bowed to his departing guests. We also bowed and returned to the machiai, where we expressed our gratitude to one another before leaving.

A painting on gold leaf by Sakai Hoitsu also captures the essence of nature.

The rings of this iron kama, or kettle for boiling tea water, are separate so it can be comfortably lifted while hot.

At this point, I discovered that I had made a serious mistake in etiquette. Early in the ceremony, I openly admired the eleventh-century (Heian Period) bronze candleholder I was using. This required the host to enclose the object in a beautiful brocade *furoshiki* (wrapper) and present it as a gift to me.

A striking moon window demonstrates principles of both wabi *and* sabi.

A Japanese landscape of this sort perhaps inspired the legendary Sun Goddess of Japan, Amaterasu Omi Kami, to remark after her creation of the islands that is was "a beautiful country."

Etiquette also demanded that a gift of like value be given to the host by the admiring recipient of such a gift at a later occasion. This can be a heavy responsibility when the object in question is a priceless museum piece. Many years after, I found an eleventh-century bronze *ewer* (bottle with long neck and spout) in a *souk* (marketplace) of Teheran, Iran, suitable for use in a tea ceremony, and I presented it to Mr. Mioshi. Later, when I attended another tea ceremony at his home, he used this object, so the debt was repaid.

This story illustrates the uniqueness of a tea ceremony and its purpose. Tea ceremonies are individual to their occasions and always bring truth to bear on some great aesthetic principle, such as the ultimate ink painting observed in this story.

THE AFTERLIFE
OF ENLIGHTENMENT

One tends to lead an "afterlife" following these enlightenments from another culture—a life often changed and modified by them. Certain autonomous reactions become regular and modify one's heretofore routinely Western-only actions.

Mount Fuji is captured here in a moment of yugen, *or subtlety.*

This dry-lacquer sculpture portrays a Zen monk in meditation.

Artificiality is shunned in favor of genuine and truthful choices in everything pertaining to personal life and its surroundings. One immediate and noticeable change is the abandonment of plastic plants and flowers and a reaction to them if used in public places. In other words, style for style's sake should give way to functional honesty or simplicity rather than complication. Creativity becomes a given in all aspects of human life and is not considered the property of the so-called "talented few." One's world becomes more asymmetrical and natural with its flow seen as a tool for solving some of life's complexities. The arts become understandable and a part of one's life. The tools and techniques of the artist lose their mystery and become friendly adjuncts in life's pursuits.

The clean-cut quality of wabi is part of this newly crafted woodwork.

As noted previously, color choices tend toward the shibui rather than the pretentious. Numbers lean toward the uneven as the symmetry of the classic and scientific Greeks give way to the numerology of the natural. In other words, one seeks out the subtle rather than the obvious.

Entertainment often devolves upon the creativity of the individual rather than reflecting an artificial exterior source such as electronic devices. The individual seeks satori as an ultimate learning experience

The venerable is sometimes realized in a symbol rather than in reality. Here we see a round stone echoing a moon window—a reminder of the mighty column for which it was once a base supporting a massive temple.

This contemporary carved-stone baptismal font is found in St. Mary's Cathedral in Tokyo.

and looks for atmospheres that promote it. Museum visitation becomes an adventure in ascertaining the satori of the artists rather than the cataloging of factual data. The omnipresent late-twentieth-century need for sound in all situations gives way to delight in quiet solitude and its opportunity for deep thought and individual satori. Last but not least comes the realization of creativity and the surprise of what happens when one is released from old preconceptions.

GLOSSARY

Some of these terms have already been defined at the point of usage in the text; however, they are all reintroduced here as a handy reference.

Andon—Floor lamp

Aware (ah wa ray)—The ability to realize nature in various moods.

Chabana—Tea master's flower arrangement

Chajin—Tea master

Chaniwa—Tea master's garden

Cha no yu—Tea ceremony

Chashitsu—Tearoom

Chozubachi—Water container for washing; wash basin

Datsuzoku—Surprise in creativity

Doyo—The eleven hottest days of summer

Fukinsei—Asymmetry

Furo—Brazier

Furoshiki—Wrapper

Furyu—Elegance, taste, refinement

Gaijin—Foreigner; literally foreign barbarian

Geisha—Female entertainers

Haiken—Appreciate

Heian—Corresponds to Medieval through Gothic periods of Western history

Hishaku—Dipper

Iki—Smart

Ikebana—Art of Japanese flower arrangement

Jimi—Proper, correct, sober (possibly dull)

Kakemono—Scroll painting in hanging style

Kama—Kettle

Kanso—Simplicity

Koicha—Thick tea

Kojin-mari—Coziness

Koko—Austerity

Machiai—Gathering place for guests at a tea ceremony

Momiji—Flaming red maple foliage

The Tori Gate at Miyamajima on the inland Sea of Japan symbolizes a gate that is always open to all, no matter the hour or season.

Nageire—Thrown-in style of ikebana

Nijiri-guchi—Teahouse door

Niwa—Japanese garden

Notan—Dark and light (chiaroscuro)

Onsen—Hot springs bath

Otemae—Preparation of tea

Raku—A type of pottery

Roji—Garden path

Roshi—Zen monk/abbot

Sabi—Beauty in age and patina; venerable

Satori—Instantaneous enlightenment

Seijaku—Quietness

Seika—Modification of the temple-style Rikka arrangements of flowers

Shakkei—Borrowed landscape

Shakyamuni—The Buddha before his enlightenment (satori)

Shibui—Essence of Japanese culture and the ultimate in taste; controlled understatement. It can relate to both aristocratic and Mingei (folk art) levels of taste.

Shiori-do—Inner gate

Shin—formal

Shinto—Original spirit beliefs of Japan, which revere nature and natural forces.

Shizen—Naturalness

Shoji—Sliding paper-covered screens

Shokyaku—Lead guest at a tea ceremony

Suitsuki—Moon, water, grass

Suki—Artistic taste

Sukiya—Tearoom

Sumi-e—Ink painting

Sutra—Buddhist scripture

Tatami—Floor mats

Tokonoma—An alcove used to display a painting or another work of art and a flower arrangement. Literally translated it means "treasure room."

Tsukubai—Water basin in a garden

Tsume—Last guest at a tea ceremony

Wabi—Solitary; concept of less is better; fresh and new

Yugen—Subtle and profound

Zabuton—Floor cushions

wabi

QUIETNESS

kanso

seijaku

SIMPLICITY

SUBTLE

静

FRESH

yugen

寂

sabi

脱

shizen

自

ASYMMETRY

NATURALNESS

古

然

俗

VENERABLE

datsuzoku

datsuzoku

SURPRISE

SURPRISE